# BYGONE HAMILTON

by

## HUGH GRIFFEN

BRIDGE AND LIBRARY, HAMILTON    VALENTINES SERIES

## LANARKSHIRE HERITAGE SERIES

ISBN 1-872074-04-9

Quarry Street circa 1933.

# INTRODUCTION

Having lived in Hamilton for thirteen years as a boy, when I was presented with the opportunity of writing this book I was fascinated by the rich and varied history of the town.

The area, at one time called Cadzow, was the ancient hunting ground of Rhyderrach, King of Strathclyde. The name of Cadzow was used until the middle of the fifteenth Century when the present day name of Hamilton was "adopted". The town became a Burgh in 1475 and received its first Member of Parliament in 1832. With an early history of battles, castles, martyrs and the Dukes of Hamilton, the town has also been one of the centres of the Scottish coal industry in more modern times.

Older readers may well remember some of the scenes shown here and I hope that the facts stated here will encourage younger readers to take an interest in the town.

Hugh Griffen, January 1990.

Bandstand, Public Park, Hamilton.

Hamilton                                    Cadzow Street

Cadzow Street was originally built to by-pass the route of Castle Street and Muir Street. This was considered to be too dangerous because of the "Devil's Elbow Corner" where many a horse and cart came to grief.

This view of Cadzow Street from the corner of Castle Street shows the different modes of transport in use at the beginning of this century. Electric trams and horses and carts are still very evident. At this time, this part of Cadzow Street was the site of the junction between Tramway No.1 and Tramway No.2 (the Larkhall branch).

5

4313 - 11. Watson Fountain, Hamilton.

The Watson Fountain, at the junction of Muir Street and Cadzow Street was presented to the Town in 1893 by Sir John Watson, Bart., a prominent local coalmaster. The sheep on the right are probably about to be driven down Muir Street to the old slaughterhouse at Sheilinghill.

*Watson Fountain, Hamilton*

Tram No.7 en route to Blantyre, stops to pick up passengers at the Watson Fountain. The car was operated by the Lanarkshire Tramways Company and was introduced in 1903, in time for the opening of services on the newly completed tram network.

Cadzow Bridge

Hamilton

Work is under progress on the Masonic Temple at the corner of Lower Auchingramont Road in this view of
Cadzow Bridge. The foundation Stone of the Temple was laid by the Lodge Master, W.P. Mitchell, on the 3rd
of September, 1903. When the trams were introduced, the arches of the bridge were suggested as the possible
site of a theatre.

8

Cadzow Bridge and Masonic Temple, Hamilton

G. Buchanan, Stationer, Hamilton.

This later view of Cadzow Bridge shows the completed Masonic Temple. On the right of the bridge is the cleared site for the new library. The bridge was built in 1835 when Cadzow Street was laid out. It was rebuilt and widened in 1900 to accommodate the trams which started running in 1903.

Masonic Temple, Hamilton

Lodge Hamilton, Kilwinning No. 7 was planned by Hamilton architect Alexander Cullen and cost £8000 to construct. The foundation stone was the original foundation stone of the old Lodge, which dated from 1816. The new Masonic Temple opened on the 27th of December, 1904.

The library was the first part of the present Town Hall and Municipal Buildings to be constructed. A grant for part of the cost of building the library was received from Andrew Carnegie, of Skibo. The library opened on the 17th of September, 1907.

"Old Town, Hamilton."

*not a very nice view but better than nothing. N. 9.*

The present day streets of Grammar School Square and Portwell now cover this part of old Hamilton. Visible in the middle background is the old Tolbooth dating from 1643. It was demolished in 1954 and the site is now one of the entrances to Strathclyde Park.

Seen from Cadzow Bridge, the area around the wool merchants is the approximate site of the old slaughterhouse. It was in operation from 1795 until 1929 when the new abbattoir was opened at Blackmuir Plantation, next to the public park. Today there is still a small cattle yard operating in this part of town. In the background, Hamilton Palace is visible, the flag indicates that the Duke was in residence at the time this photograph was taken.

Work began on Hamilton Parish Church in 1729, and it opened for worship in 1734. It was built on ground donated by Thomas Aikman. In the grounds stands the original Netherton Cross as well as a memorial to four Covenanter martyrs; John Parker, Gavin Hamilton, James Hamilton and Christopher Strang, who were executed at Edinburgh on the seventh of December, 1666. Their heads were later set up at the Tolbooth, Overtoun and their right hands displayed on the public ports at Lanark, where they had taken the Covenant.

Located in the old palace grounds, the Bishop's Gate no longer exists. It appeared to have no clerical connections and was purely ornamental.

Hamilton Palace dates from 1591 but had a host of alterations and additions made to it by successive Dukes. This view shows the portico of the main front, taken from what was the North Avenue. The Avenue ran from the Palace to Bothwellhaugh and terminated on the other side of the Clyde. The Palace was ready for demolition in 1922 but the process took eight years to complete. During these eight years various parts of the Palace were used to house homeless families.

Chatelherault                                                                    Hamilton

Like the parish church, the hunting lodge of Chatelherault was designed by William Adam. The building was commissioned by James the Fifth Duke, work began in 1732 and was not completed until 1744. Eventually, through neglect and the effects of subsidence, the building fell into disrepair. Chatelherault has now been restored to its former glory and it is now the centrepiece of the Country Park, which opened on the 30th September, 1987.

Standing in the north west corner of the High Parks, this monument was erected by the tenants and friends of William, the 11th Duke of Hamilton, who died in 1863. The site was chosen by his wife, Princess Marie of Baden. Although the monument is still there, the bust of the Duke is now situated in the visitor centre at Chatelherault.

Another feature of the High Parks is the herd of wild white cattle. This is the last true herd of wild cattle in Britain and is thought to be descended from the wild cattle which roamed the Caledonian Forest at the time of the Romans. As well as the living cattle, there are two specimens preserved in the public library.

AVON BRIDGE, NEAR HAMILTON. (7)                                              215701. J.V.

The old Avon Bridge, is a three span bridge of dressed stone. The date of construction or the origin of the bridge are unknown, although it is reputed to be as old as Bothwell Bridge. Conflicting accounts state that it was built by a rich priest for his own convenience, or by monks at Lesmahagow after some of them drowned attempting to ford the river. Today, the bridge carries a private road.

20

This bridge was designed by the famous Scottish engineer Thomas Telford and was constructed as part of the Glasgow/Carlisle road improvements in 1820. The Avon Mill, shown on the right, was once owned by the Dukes of Hamilton and was gifted to the town in 1725. The age of the mill is uncertain but thought to be early 17th Century. The mill was destroyed by fire in 1963.

Townhead School, now Barncluith Primary, was opened in 1875 at Broken Cross. In the foreground Robert McGhie's bakery van poses catching a free advertisement in this c.1904 view. The origin of the name Broken Cross is unknown, but it is formed by the junctions of Miller Street, Townhead Street, Carlisle Road and Barncluith Road. Miller Street was named after local yarn merchant John Miller and was laid out in 1754.

TOWNHEAD STREET, HAMILTON

Townhead Street circa 1905 in a postcard by Glasgow publisher William Love.
Thanks to C. Neilson of Hamilton and all others who wrote regarding the original caption.

The Cross, Hamilton

This view of Townhead Street dates from early in the First World War and shows Car No.45, bound for Larkhall. In the foreground the window of the rifle range displays the notice "We want a nation of shooters, not shouters."

THE CROSS, HAMILTON

Decorations for the coronation of King George VI fix the date of this photograph to May 1937. Note that all traces of the tramlines and pylons have now been removed.

OLD CROSS, HAMILTON.

219534.

Just around the corner from Townhead Street, this is the end of Quarry Street, looking on to Keith Street. The La Scala Cinema, which opened on 14th March 1921, is clearly visible in Keith Street. In 1948 its name was changed to the Gaumont which closed on 5th November 1960. On 1st July 1961, it reopened as the Gaumont Top Rank Bingo and Social Club, later becoming the Vogue Bingo Club. Adjacent to the cinema is the Salon which became the Splendid Restaurant in 1963. A building project is underway on the site at the time of writing.

QUARRY STREET, HAMILTON.    A9400.

The end of Quarry Street was known as "the neck o' the bottle". Property here was acquired by the council in 1911 at a cost of around £8,000 in order to widen the street. In 1927 when the Burton's shop was built at the end of the street it was set back from the original line of the buildings. Quarry Street was originally named Quarry Lane as it ran to the Donaghadee Quarry which dates from 1637.

In this late 1920's view of the New Cross the old town hall still has its steeple. McGregor's Newsagent & Toy Emporium still occupies the building on the left. The A.E.C. bus on the right belonged to the Lanarkshire Tramway Company and was licensed to run anywhere in Lanarkshire between August, 1928 and June, 1929.

NEW CROSS, HAMILTON.

In 1928 the new Town Hall opened in Lower Auchingramont Road. The old Town Hall was closed, and is shown here after the steeple was taken down. Part of the modern shopping precinct is located where the old Town Hall stood, and the British Linen Bank building is now a building society.

Another feature of the New Cross was the Royal Hotel and Royal Bar. The Bar later closed and became the British Linen Bank. Little has changed structurally at the corner of New Cross since this photograph was published in 1904.

Another view of the Royal Hotel taken at the same time as the previous photograph. This, and many other pictures in this book, are from the "Brandon Series" of postcards, published by the Hamilton Herald Company. The series began in 1903 and covers much of northern Lanarkshire and Glasgow.

31

Low Waters was a separate village until 1878 when the burgh boundaries were extended to include it within Hamilton.

Eddlewood Workmen's Bowling Green was opened in 1908. The Green was built and laid out by miners from local collieries and was exclusively for their own use. Today the pavilion has been replaced by a more modern structure.

View of Race Course from Grandstand, Hamilton Racecourse

C 75

Hamilton Racecourse was formerly part of the Duke of Hamilton's Parks. The first recorded race was held there in 1782, but modern racing did not start there until 1888.

HAMILTON. ACADEMICAL. F. C.

Back Row: J. Simpson (Trainer). S. G. Baxter (Secretary). W. McLaughlin. W. Wilson (Director). J. Atkinson. J. Freeman. J. Davie. A. Govans (Director). J. Waugh. J. Scott. J. Ramsay (Assistant Trainer). T. Dodd (Director). T Moore (Director). Front Row: J. Irvine. M. Moran. G. King. W. Daziel (Chairman). W. Brownlie. R. Mason. J. Stewart.

[Photo by W. B. Dickson, Hamilton.

Still in a sporting vein, the Hamilton Academicals team of the 1910-11 season. The Club was founded in 1875 by James Blacklock, rector of Hamilton Academy, as a school team. The club played on several local pitches before moving to its present home at Douglas Park in 1888. The team went professional in 1893, they are the only professional side in Britain to have originated from a school team.

35

Records of a school in Hamilton date back to the late 16th Century when a school was located in the Palace grounds, just east of the Collegiate Church. In 1714, the Duchess Anne had a replacement built in Grammar School Square, which was demolished in 1931. The title "Academy" was first used for the school which opened in Hope Street in 1848. In 1876 the Academy was taken over by the School Board and moved to Woodside School in 1900. Construction of the new Academy began in 1910 and it was opened in 1913. It is now part of Hamilton Grammar School.

*Gilbertfield School, Hamilton, Scotland, in which Fred. S. Arnot as a boy of 6 Years heard his first call to Africa from the lips of David Livingstone.*

DAVID LIVINGSTONE

FRED S. ARNOT when 6 years old.

The earliest record of Gilbertfield is on a map of 1819, and was at that time the residence of a Mr. Mather who lived there until 1847. Attached to St. John's Church in 1834, it was run by the Church until 1896 when the School Board took over. It was subsequently gifted to the Y.M.C.A. who used it until 1964. Situated in High Patrick Street, it fell victim to the modernisation taking place in the town centre.

A fine view of the Established Church, Burnbank, photographed prior to the First World War and published by local newsagent, Dickson of Burnbank.

Photographed on the 19th of January, 1903, Tram No.20 out on trial testing the lines and power wires. The tram was built by the British Electric Car Company and was operated by Thompson Houston Co., who operated trams all over Britain.

Baxter's Bus Service of Blantyre used this new 1928 Leyland Lion PLSC1, with seating for thirty-one passengers, to compete with the Glasgow General Omnibus Company. One of their buses, an "Associated Daimler" also new that year, is shown just in the picture. Baxter's (which had no connection with Baxter's of Airdrie, apart from the family name) was taken over in 1929 by J. W. & R. Torrance Limited of Hamilton. VA 7941 had a relatively short life, and was scrapped in 1934.

40 *(Caption by George Waugh, Glasgow)*

The Barracks date back to 1795 when the grazing grounds at Bothwell Road were feued to the Crown. The Barracks were primarily used to house cavalry but they were withdrawn from Hamilton in 1877 when the new Barracks opened at Maryhill in Glasgow.

Over the years the Barracks have been the home of the 26th Cameronians (Scottish Rifles) and the 73rd, 74th and 90th Highland Regiments. Adjoining the Barracks were the headquarters of the 16th Lanarkshire Rifle Volunteers of the 1st Royal Lanark Militia. After falling into disrepair, the Barracks were demolished in 1967. Bell College now stands on the site. This postcard shows a mounted detachment of the Lanarkshire Constabulary in December 1909. From left to right, the police officers are Constables Farquhar, Rose, Wood, Nicolson, Inspector Kemp, Sergeant Instructor Davis, and Constables Baird, McBean, Kimmond and Sutherland.

Peacock Cross takes its name from a small croft which stood on the site, which was in the ownership of a man named Peacock. The croft disappeared in 1841 when the Cambuslang Road Trustees obtained powers to create a new road joining Burnbank Road to Brandon Street. This is now the present day Union Street. The corner building at the Cross is now the Peacock Tavern.

The houses at the corner of Burnbank Road and Dalziel Street have now all gone and have been replaced by small industrial units.

Dating from 1903, this view shows Burnbank Cross. In front of the confectioners is a decorative lamp-post and fountain. Tram No.17 is heading towards Wishaw.

Photographed about ten years later, the Cross has altered little; Wilson's the confectioners has become a bank and the first motor vehicles have appeared. The area is barely recognisable today through redevelopment.

The Gilmour Memorial Church and Burnbank Library are both still features of Glasgow Road. The library was opened on Monday, the 31st of January, 1955 by Baillie Adam Russell. Originally the Police Station, the building was converted for use as a library at a total cost of £1950.

This is one of a series of cards of Burnbank, published by William Love of Glasgow. It shows Glasgow Road looking towards the corner of Glenlee Street.

Burnbank Station, N.B.

Burnbank Railway station was situated just next to Bertram Street. The line was opened by the Glasgow, Bothwell, Hamilton & Coatbridge Railway Company on the 1st of April, 1878 and was operated from the beginning by the North British Railway. This Company took over the line totally on the 2nd of August, 1878.

Railway and Footbridge, Hamilton.

Part of the same line, this foot and rail bridge crossed the Wellshaw Burn.

In 1854 Glenlee House was owned by Alexander Miller, and was later the residence of Lewis Potter, who was jailed when the City of Glasgow Bank collapsed in 1878. In that year J. Clelland, Chairman of the Cunard Steamship Company bought the mansion. Around the turn of the Century it became a Tuberculosis Hospital. It was later used as Walter McGowan's Training Gym, but by March 1971 was being used to store furniture prior to its demolition.

*Glenlee Public School, Burnbank, Hamilton.*

Glenlee School took its name from Glenlee House in the previous picture. The school was built during the Boer War in 1901. After falling victim to subsidence caused by the extensive mine workings in the area, it was shored up for a number of years and eventually replaced by the present building in 1964.

Earnock House, Hamilton.

The first records of private ownership of the Earnock Estate date back to the Tenth Century, when Robertus Robertoun held the title. In more modern times the estate was purchased by Sir John Watson Bart., a local coalmaster, from the trustees of a Mrs. Williams. Repairs were undertaken in 1874 and completed the following year. Electric light was introduced to the house and the nearby Earnock Colliery in 1881, although the town of Hamilton did not receive electricity until 1903. The house was sold by Sir John's eldest son (the second Sir John) in 1925 and demolition work commenced during 1926.

Thanks are due to Lt. Col. Sir John Inglefield-Watson Bart, for providing extra information.

EARNOCK COLLIERY BURNBANK

Earnock Colliery was opened by Sir John Watson Bart., in 1877 and the first coal produced in late 1879. One of the first pithead signs forbidding smoking was introduced after the tragic explosion at the Blantyre Pit on the 22nd October, 1877. The colliery was situated just off the present Hillhouse Road, between Wellhall Road and Hill Street. Earnock Colliery closed on the 18th of April, 1942, after the coal seams became exhausted.

*Left:* These gates formed one entrance to the Bent Cemetery, which opened in 1853.

*Right:* This circa 1910 photograph shows Lovers Lane in the Low Waters area. The Lane was a right of way and ran from Tuphall Road to Mill Road past two small quarries. The scene shown here totally disappeared when the houses at Alness Street were built between 1926 and 1927.

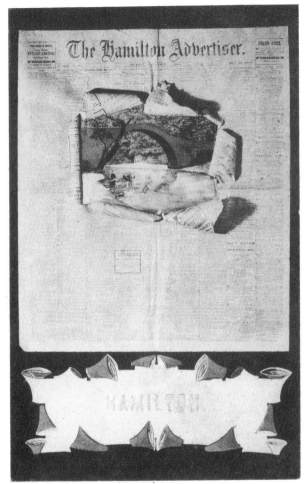

Published by Hills of Sunderland, this postcard shows the Roman Bridge at Strathclyde Country Park. This series, using the front page from local newspapers, covered many small towns in Scotland and northern England.

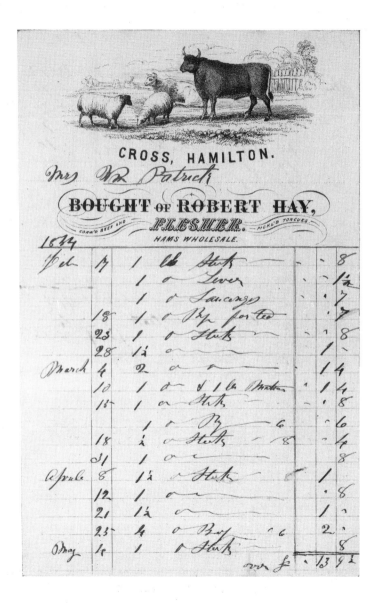